Spitsbergen july 2 [illegible]

To Ann,

best wishes from the author!

(when do you come up here?)

Rinie

POLAR ODYSSEY

Voyages in the Arctic and Antarctic

Photography
Rinie van Meurs

GMB *uitgeverij / Oceanwide Expeditions / Pica Press*

ISBN 90-74345-31-X (NL)
ISBN 1-903206-00-6 (UK)

NUGI 470

Oceanwide Expeditions is the corporate sponsor of Macaroni Penguin *Eudyptes chrysolophus* in BirdLife International's *'Threatened Birds of the World'*, part of BirdLife's Globally Threatened Species Programme.

COLOFON

Text & photography: *Rinie van Meurs, Rosmalen (NL)*
English translation: *Ingrid Visser, Whangarei (NZ)*
Editor: *Ger Meesters, Haarlem (NL)*
Colour separation: *René Pop, Julianadorp (NL)*
Design & lay-out: *Studio Kisteman, Julianadorp (NL)*
Printing: *South Sea International Press Ltd., Hong Kong*
Publishers:
- *Ger Meesters Boekproducties Vrijheidsweg 86, NL-2033 Haarlem*
- *Oceanwide Expeditions Bellamypark 9, NL-4381 CG Vlissingen tel. 00-31-118-410410 www.ocnwide.com*
- *Pica Press The Banks, Mountfield, nr. Robertsbridge East-Sussex TN32 5JY, UK*

Acknowledgments

In the past years I have made many voyages and expeditions for Oceanwide Expeditions mainly to the Antarctic and Arctic. These voyages gave me the opportunity to practise my nature photography. In front of you is my second photo-book, a beautiful result which would not have been possible without the help and advice from a number of people. Herewith I would like express my thanks to all these friends for their support and advice.

- **Michel van Gessel**, Director of Oceanwide Expeditions, who is responsible for the organisation of all the voyages for which I was Expedition Leader. Most of the pictures in this book have been taken during these voyages.
- **Ko de Korte**, an old friend, from whom I've learnt a lot about travelling in polar regions. Thanks to him I became involved in the world of expedition style cruises.
- **René Pop**, one of my best friends, he is also a photographer and lithographer, with whom I could always share my enthusiasm for travel and nature photography through all these years. Together with him I made the selection of photos for this book.
- **Ingrid Visser**, long-time soulmate and travel companion. Ingrid translated the text into English. She introduced me to the fascinating underwater world and her marine mammal friends.
- All the **employees** in the Office of Oceanwide Expeditions who kept the home port running and gave full support to me out in the field so the voyages ran smoothly.
- All **colleagues** with whom I sailed, who became friends through the years, in particular **Martin Gray**, who often gave me his support and advice during our Arctic cruises.
- **John Neuschwander, Greg Mortimer, Albert Beintema** & **Robert (Bob) Headland** for their contributions.
- The **Crew** of the **Professor Molchanov** for their professionalism and their efficiency which made the operations run smoothly and safely.
- All **passengers** who sailed with me in the past and with whom I had the pleasure of sharing my experiences. To all future passengers, for whom the adventure is yet to come.
- The last in this list, but certainly not the least of importance, my dearest **Parents**, who always supported and inspired me to extend my horizons to every corner of this planet.

Rinie van Meurs

The expedition ship, the Professor Molchanov:

'A character in Antarctic and Arctic Oceans.'

Preface

'Every day and night,
my heart is longing for discovering unknown countries.
To tell stories in later life.
One's wasting of precious time, would scarcely be more disgraceful than a young man
remaining under mothers wings, or the ordinary good-for-nothing,
for they will never comprehend the difference between poverty and wealth, nor what the
world has to offer.'

This passage, written by a young 20 year old Dutchman in 1583[1] is one of the many examples of the exploratory attitude of the West-Europeans in the period of the great discoveries. Initiated by Columbus and the Portuguese sailors Vasco da Gama and Magalhaes other countries also began to explore the New World. In their attempts to reach the Indies, the Dutch choose for an Arctic route and in 1596 Willem Barentsz encountered a land he called 'the new land of Spitsbergen.' In the centuries that followed, explorers like William Parry (England, 1827), Frederick Cook (USA, 1908) and Roald Amundsen (Norway, 1926) made attempts to set foot on the North Pole. Amundsen reaching the pole in December 1911 won the 'battle of the Antarctic.'

Apart from economical interests and status, these brave enterprises could not have taken place without some crucial key motives: curiosity and the eagerness to explore. Although the terrestrial side of the world is nearly completely discovered, these inducements are still implied in what we call exploration travel. In 1981 the predecessor of Oceanwide Expeditions offered the first commercial expedition cruise to Spitsbergen. Since 1996 Oceanwide has been offering year-round-programs with comfortable Russian ice-strengthened vessels in both the Arctic and the Antarctic. Voyages on which our passengers can explore untouched nature and relive the experiences of the very first adventurers.

With the first discoveries information and knowledge were brought to the ignorant home front. Maps appeared of the New World, paintings visualised the unknown, supported by travelogues. Photography undoubtedly increased the imaginative faculty. One of the most significant photographers was Frank Hurley, who participated in one of the British Antarctic expeditions of Ernest Shackleton in 1915. The vessel he had sailed South on got stuck in the ice and the team had to return with a wooden sloop. In order to limit luggage Hurley had to select no more than 120 glass-negatives, the others were left behind. Nowadays, no single traveller is embarking our vessels without a camera, shooting between 500 and 1,000 pictures per voyage. Travellers simply have the desire to store and perpetuate their travel experiences. In this case, not much has been changed since the 20 year old Dutchman wrote in 1583 that he wishes to explore in order to tell stories in later life.

This exceptional book, of our expedition leader and very dear friend Rinie van Meurs, is highly recommended to those who love, and has or will visit the Polar and Atlantic areas. It is without question a must for every modern storyteller.

Vlissingen, 1 april 2000

Michel van Gessel
Managing Director of Oceanwide Expeditions

A. and H. Algra, Despereert niet. Twintig eeuwen historie van de Nederlanden, deel 4 (Don't despair. Twenty ages of history of the Netherlands), Franeker 1956

The Arctic

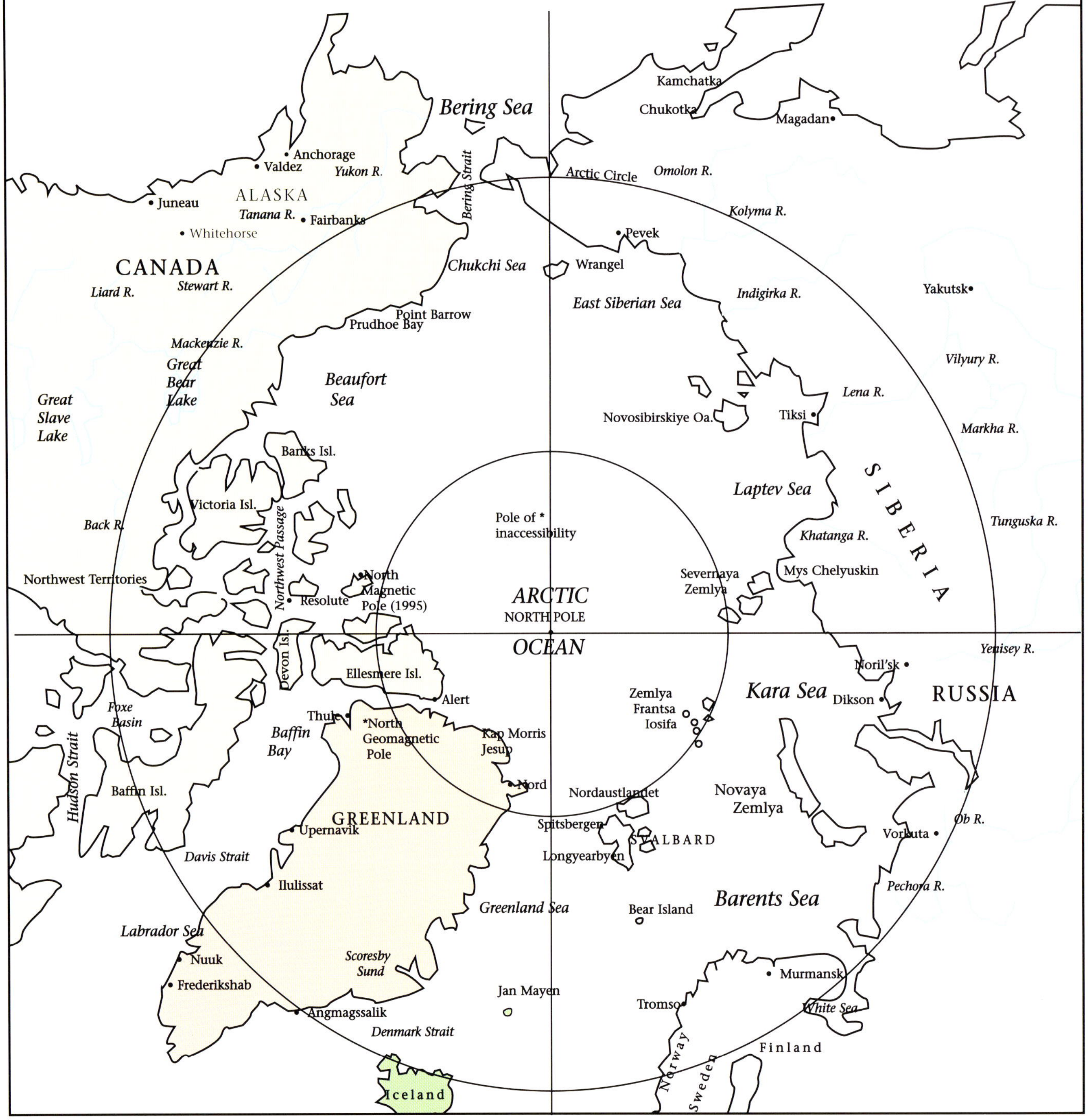
Bering Sea
Kamchatka
Chukotka
Magadan
Anchorage
Valdez
Yukon R.
Bering Strait
Arctic Circle
Omolon R.
Juneau
ALASKA
Tanana R.
Fairbanks
Whitehorse
Kolyma R.
Pevek
CANADA
Stewart R.
Liard R.
Chukchi Sea
Wrangel
Yakutsk
Point Barrow
Prudhoe Bay
East Siberian Sea
Indigirka R.
Mackenzie R.
Great Bear Lake
Beaufort Sea
Vilyury R.
Great Slave Lake
Lena R.
Novosibirskiye Oa.
Tiksi
Markha R.
Banks Isl.
Laptev Sea
SIBERIA
Victoria Isl.
Pole of inaccessibility
Back R.
Northwest Passage
Tunguska R.
Khatanga R.
Northwest Territories
North Magnetic Pole (1995)
Resolute
ARCTIC
NORTH POLE
OCEAN
Severnaya Zemlya
Mys Chelyuskin
Devon Isl.
Ellesmere Isl.
Yenisey R.
Noril'sk
Alert
Zemlya Frantsa Iosifa
Kara Sea
Dikson
RUSSIA
Foxe Basin
Thule
*North Geomagnetic Pole
Baffin Bay
Kap Morris Jesup
Hudson Strait
Baffin Isl.
Nord
Nordaustlandet
Novaya Zemlya
GREENLAND
Upernavik
Spitsbergen
SVALBARD
Ob R.
Vorkuta
Davis Strait
Longyearbyen
Ilulissat
Pechora R.
Barents Sea
Greenland Sea
Bear Island
Labrador Sea
Nuuk
Scoresby Sund
Murmansk
Frederikshab
Jan Mayen
Tromso
White Sea
Angmagssalik
Denmark Strait
Finland
Norway
Sweden
Iceland

The Arctic

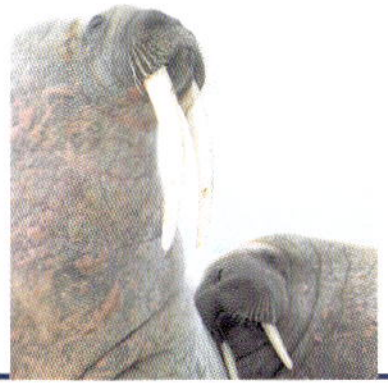

The Arctic is essentially an ocean (the smallest), the northern extremities of three continents and several archipelagos. The boundaries are not distinct, but are best defined by a combination of the tree-line, the southern limit of continuous permafrost, and the average extent of winter sea ice.

The Arctic Ocean includes the Barents Sea, Kara Sea, Laptev Sea, East Siberian Sea, Chukchi Sea, Beaufort Sea, and Lincoln Sea. It receives a large fresh-water influx from many of the world's greatest rivers. Its surface area is 14,5 million km^2 of which a summer minimum of 50% is permanently covered by sea ice; this increases to 85% in winter. The mean ice thickness is 3 m; the average duration of a floe is 3 years. At the North Pole it may drift as much as 20 km daily. The greatest oceanic depth is 5502 m and the depth at the North Pole is 4420 m (the ice reaches about 0,5 m above the sea). Its submarine topography is complex. The remote Northern Pole of Inaccessibility is at 84.05°N, 174.85°W, 1100 km from the nearest coast.

The climate is extreme but the low altitude and proximity of the sea ameliorate it compared with that of the Antarctic. Winds may be severe and precipitation, mainly snow, is generally abundant. Nord station, on north-east Greenland, has recorded a minimum near -70°C. Arctic flora and fauna are closely related to those of surrounding continents but have adapted to the harsh climate. Polar Bear and Ringed Seals have been found north of 88°N. Migratory birds occupy breeding sites in immense number during the summer.

Eight countries govern Arctic Regions which co-ordinate various projects between themselves and several others which participate. Scientific co-operation is largely accomplished through the International Arctic Science Committee.

The People The Arctic has had a peripheral indigenous population for many thousand years. These include tribes of Eskimo, Lapp, Samoyeds, and Chukchi. Settlements have existed north of 80°N in Greenland. About 80% of the present population immigrated during the last century and established population centres.

Exploration of the continental land was largely complete almost two centuries ago, but the last of the islands was not discovered until 1947.

The North Pole was first seen on 12 May 1926, from an airship, but not reached until 23 April 1948. Sealers, whalers, hunters, and trappers have been long established in the Arctic. Extraction of metals and hydrocarbons is a major activity. many air and sea routes cross the Arctic and tourism is small but increasing. Russia maintains the Northern Sea Route with a fleet of icebreakers, some nuclear-powered.

Polar stations, from many countries conduct research and maintain observatories around the Arctic Ocean, on islands and adrift. Many military stations exist although numbers have been reduced since 1991. Novaya Zemlya has been a major atomic bomb testing site.

Greenland has the largest Arctic ice sheet with an area of 1.8 million km^2 and a volume of 2.5 million km^3 which is 9% of the ice on Earth. The greatest depth known is 3350 m and average depth 1200 m. Bedrock is depressed to a maximum depth of 450 m below sea level. Greenland also has the highest peak in the Arctic: Gunnbjørns Fjæld at 3693 m (68.92°N, 29.90°W, first climbed on 18 August 1935). The many Arctic ice caps are of comparatively minor size; no large ice shelves exist.

R.K. Headland
Scott Polar Research Institute

Concise chronology of approach to the North Pole

The following list give explorations, in chronological order, towards the North Pole, their attainment (by sea, air and surface), and the first crossings of the region. There are several claims includes for which supporting evidence is unsatisfactory and doubts exist about their accomplishments.

1553 Sir Hugh Willoughby (England), with companies aboard Bona Esperanza and Bona Confidentia, reached 72°N on the Novaya Zemlya coast, 14 August.

1587 John Davis (England), with companies aboard Elizabeth, Ellen, and Sunshine, reached 72.20°N off Greenland, July.

1594 Willem Barentsz (Netherlands), with a ship's company, reached 77°N rounding Novaya Zemlya, July.

1596 Jacob van Heemskerck (Netherlands), with companies aboard 2 vessels, reached 80.18°N of Svalbard, 17 June.

1607 Henry Hudson (Britain), with company aboard Hopewell, reached 80.38°N off Svalbard, 16 July.

1766 Vasiliy Chichagov (Russia), with companies aboard Chichagov, Panov and Babayev, reached 80.47°N off Svalbard, 16 July.

1773 Constantine Phipps (Britain), with companies aboard Racehorse and Carcass, reached 80.80°N, 27 July Subsequently many whaling vessels reached high latitudes.

1806 William Scoresby (Britain), with company aboard Resolution, reached 81.50°N, off Svalbard.

1827 William Parry (Britain) and party, with two sledge boats from Hecla, reached 82.75°N off Svalbard, 25 July This position is farther north than the area inhabited by the Polar Eskimo of Greenland.

1876 Albert Markham (Britain) and 2 sledge parties reached 83.34°N off Ellesmere Island, 12 May.

1882 James Lockwood (United States) and 2 others dog-sledged to 83.40°N off Greenland from Fort Conger, 13 May

1895 Fridtjof Nansen and Hjalmar Johansen (Norway) dog-sledged to 86.22°M from Fram in the Arctic Ocean, 8 April.

1900 Umberto Cagni (Italy) and 3 others claimed to have dog-sledged to 86.57°N from Zemlya Frantsa-Iosefa, 24 April

1908 Frederick Cook (United States), with a sledge party, claimed to have reached 90°N, 21 April.

1909 Robert Peary (United States) and an expeditionary party, dog-sledged to 87.75°N from Ellesmere Island, 31 March, Peary and 5 others continued north and possibly passed 88°N.

1909 Robert Peary (United States), with a sledge party, claimed to have reached 90°N, 6 April.

1925 Roald Amundsen (Norway), Lincoln Ellsworth (United States) and 4 others flew north from Svalbard in 2 aircraft, crash landed and drifted to 87.83°N, 21 May.

1926 Richard Byrd (United States), with an aircraft crew, claimed to have reached 90°N by air from Svalbard, 9 May.

1926 Roald Amundsen (Norway), Lincoln Ellsworth (United States), Umberto Nobile (Italy) and 11 others, crossed 90°N by airship Norge (flying Svalbard to Alaska), 12 May. Subsequently one dirigible balloon and many other aircraft have flown over the North Pole.

1937 Ivan Papanin (Soviet Union) and party landed at 89.43°N by aircraft from Zemlya Frantsa Iosefa, established the first Arctic Ocean drift station, 21 May.

1948 Pavel Gordiyenko (Soviet Union) and 5 others, landed at 90°N from an air craft, 23 April. Subsequently many aircraft have landed at the North Pole.

1958 John Anderson (United States), with crew aboard nuclear powered submarine USS Nautilus, reached the North Pole while submerged, 3 August, on voyage from the Pacific Ocean to the Atlantic Ocean.

1959 James Calvert (United States, with crew aboard nuclear powered submarine USS Skate, surfaced at the North Pole, 17 March. Subsequently many submarines reached the North Pole and some surfaced there.

1968 Ralph Plaisted (United States) and 3 others reached 90°N by surface (snow scooter) from Canada, and returned by air, 19 April.

1969 Wally Herbert (Britain) and 3 others dog-sledged to 90°N, while crossing the Arctic Ocean (Alaska to Svalbard), 6 April. Subsequent several expeditions have crossed the Arctic on the pack-ice through the North Pole and many have made one-way surface journeys leaving by air.

1977 Yuriy Kuchiyev (Soviet Union), with crew aboard nuclear powered icebreaker Arktika, reached 90°N by sea from near the Novosibirskiye Ostrova, 17 August. Subsequently many surface vessels have reached the North Pole.

1981 The predecessors of Oceanwide Expeditions (Plancius Foundation, Amsterdam) organised the very first expedition cruise with m/v Plancius to Spitsbergen.

1991 Anatoly Gorshkovskiy (Soviet Union), with crew and passengers aboard the nuclear powered icebreaker Sovetskiy Soyuz, reached the North Pole by sea while crossing the Arctic Ocean (Murmansk to Provideniya), 4 August.

The spectacular cliffs of the Scottish Islands are the nesting sites for thousands of sea birds.

Gannets, *Morus bassanus,* (above) spend their winter at sea but come back in early spring to start their breeding season. To strengthen the pairbond they spend a lot of time socializing and preening each other.

Atlantic Puffins, *Fratercula arctica,* prefer grassy slopes, in which they dig burrows for their nests. On some islands these birds are still considered a delicacy.

Kittiwakes, *Rissa tridactyla*, displaying at the nest.
Before building their nest, they often dip their nestmaterial in fresh water!

The Shag, *Stictocarbo aristotelis,* is a typical inhabitant of the Scottish Islands.

View of the Faroe Islands

Crevices, in rocky cliffs, are the ideal breeding site for the Razorbill, *Alca torda*. Here the eggs or young birds are save for predators like skuas.

A view of the *Berenberg* on Jan Mayen. In the foreground the *Brielse toren* (named after the Dutch town Brielle by Dutch whalers.

Remains of blubber ovens on Amsterdam Island of Spitsbergen, from the Dutch whaling period in the 17th Century.

Monaco Glacier. The islands of Spitsbergen ('pointed mountains') got its name from the mountains behind the glacier.

Northern Fulmars, *Fulmarus glacialis,* in the high Arctic are usually darker than their conspecifics in the British Islands. They are more closely related to the albatrosses than to the gulls.

The skeleton of a bowhead whale, *Balaena mysticetus* (above). The whaling period on Spitsbergen started in 1612. In the beginning it was mainly for the oil which was rendered from the thick layer of fat on the whales (blubber). The most famous whaling station was Smeerenburg ('Blubbertown') on Amsterdam Island.

Spiderplant, *Saxifraga flagellaris*, one of the many beautiful plants in the Arctic.

The Long-tailed Skua, *Stercorarius longicaudus* is an opportunist which feeds on lemmings, (*Lemmus sp.*), but it also breeds on Spitsbergen, where lemmings are absent. It has a magnificent flight with its unmistakable long tailfeathers

The Barnacle Goose, *Branta leucopsis,* is a typical bird of the high Arctic. In the winter it migrates south to western Europe, where huge flocks can be found in Scotland and the Netherlands. The young stay with their parents until they return to the breeding grounds.

Walruses, *Odobenus rosmarus,* were heavily hunted for their ivory in the past. Due to protection by several countries they are slowly recovering. Walrus eat molluscs (shellfish) that live on the sea floor, especially the 'blunt-gapper', *Mya truncata,* which seems to be their favourite. In the past it was thought that the tusks were used to dig, but now it is known that they use their whiskers to discover the shellfish hidden in the sand. Males and females live in separate herds, year round. However they meet briefly in February for mating. The calf is born 15 months later.

The short summer and the perma-frost are important factors that limit the vegetation in the high Arctic. The upper layer of earth thaws in summer and provides enough water and nutrients for plants to survive, so it is often called the active layer. Arctic cotton grass, *Eriphorum scheuchzeri,* (left), grows in high moisture areas. The moss campion, *Silene acaulis,* creates a thick cushion. The temperature in the cushion is higher than the surrounding temperature, which stimulates growth.

Displaying Eider duck (drake), *Somateria mollissima.*

The Little Auk, *Alle alle,* is the most abundant bird in the high Arctic. It nests on scree slopes, in small crevices and holes. It feeds on small crustaceans (shrimp-like creatures) which they collect in their crop to take to the chicks.

(page 24) Cape Tegetthoff on Franz Josephland. The typical rock formation in the background was drawn in 1874 by the explorer Julius von Payer, who discovered Franz Josef Land.

(page 25) Polar bear tracks on Bell Island, Franz Josephland.

A Reindeer stag, *Rangiferus tarandus,* just before the rutting season. He still has to clean the 'velvet' off his antlers.

Pelagic Hunt

'The ship slowly approached the wall of ice of the Monaco Glacier. Suddenly we discovered two polar bears swimming in the water – a female and her cub. From their behaviour we could see that they had a purpose. But what? It soon became clear... in the panorama of blue ice walls, screaming kittiwakes, towering mountains, and floating ice, a bearded seal was hunting for fish. Every now and then the female bear would lift her head high, looking for the seal. When she spotted it she would swim with stealth, like a hunting crocodile, as only her nose and ears protruded above the water. Instinctively the cub stayed at a distance. When the female bear was about 20 meters from the seal she dove completely under. There was great anticipation, waiting to see what would happen... suddenly she emerged, right next to the seal, wildly lunging out to hit her prey. *She missed!* But it was close, and only the murky water had saved the seal. How had she judged the distance so well? Did she learn this technique of hunting from her mother? Is she is ever successful? We will never know. But in any case, we had the chance to witness a very special hunting method which very few people had ever seen.'

Ingrid N. Visser

The Sorgfjord ('Worry Fjord'), in the northeast of Spitsbergen. During the war between the French and the Dutch, the Dutch whalers were worried when they were attacked by French Men-of-War ships, and driven into the fjord.

Purple Saxifrage, *Saxifraga oppositifolia,* (left) the most common flower in the Arctic. It even grows at 85^{0} Northern latitude, in Greenland

Storfjorden

Conflict between a Sabine's Gull, *Larus sabini,* and an Arctic Tern *Sterna paradisaea*.

Brünnich's Guillemots, *Uria lomvia,* nest on steep cliffs to be safe from their main predator, the Arctic fox. The adult birds can only bring one fish at a time, to their young. After about three weeks, they can not provide enough food for the fast growing chick. The chick (which cannot fly) will be encouraged to leap off the cliff (sometimes more than 100 m). It will then join the father and swim to the fishing grounds. So, instead of bringing the fish to the chick, which is very inefficient, they bring the chick to the fish!

The 'Professor Molchanov' in drift-ice.

The only moving things in this over-whelming, unreal landscape seem to be us, in our padded anoraks – small coloured dots, like pin heads, upon a back ground of slowly wafting mist steadily covering the mountains.
Little by little the snow begins to fall. The wind increases and the little whaler's hut appears, where we had already signed the visitors book on the outward journey. We were the first visitors to this island for a long time. And again the fog thickens.
At any moment you expect a polar bear to emerge out of the mist.
The longer the return trip – the stronger the wind and the snow – the more we sink into it – the faster my heart beats.
Presently the overpowering feeling fills me. Here I have discovered the 'window' (to the 'beyond', 'the absolute', the 'real me').

Leonie Konietzko

Arctic Terns, *Sterna paradisaea,* nest in the Arctic and spend the winter in the sub-Antarctic.

(page 35) The 14th of July Glacier is named after the national day in France.

The female Grey Phalarope, *Phalaropus fulicarius*, has brighter plumage than the male. The male incubates the eggs and raises the chicks.

The only pure white gull, is the Ivory Gull, *Pagophila eburnea*. It spends winter and summer in the vicinity of the pack ice. In the winter it often follows polar bears to scavenge scraps.

'At Mushamna we saw a polar bear! Amazing! Very exciting. We were just wandering along towards the trappers hut when it appeared a few hundred meters away. It did not seem to see us and sauntered along the shore, then it sniffed around the hut for a while before ambling off. It was certainly a different perspective to see it so close, when we were also on foot – it sent a wave of anticipation through the group – but at the same time we felt quite confident as we were in a large group...'

Greg Mortimer

Mountain Avens, *Dryas octopetala,* grows where the snow covering in winter is thin, and the water drainage in the summer is sufficient.

Fighting Brünnich's Guillemots, *Uria lomvia.*

Brünnich's Guillemots, *Uria lomvia,* resting like penguins on an iceberg.

Only a small part of an iceberg protrudes above the water.
The biggest part of the 'crystal world' stays hidden under the surface.
© Photo John Neuschwander

"You can experience an astounding underwater world through diving, dipping into laminar – forests, fully alive. Steep cliffs crowded with sea-anemones, urchins wandering the pebble floors – and you can watch some fishes – the seawolf and the scorpionfish. Diving in the pack-ice has it's own peculiar fascination – you feel like you are flying under the ice, with light and colour at play."

Regine Frerichs

An Arctic Fox, *Alopex lagopus,* harasses a Pink-footed Goose, *Anser brachyrhynchus,* on the nest, as it tries to steal the eggs. Unfortunately for the fox, the geese are able to withstand these attacks.

Bearded Seals, *Erignathus barbatus*, are on top of the menu for polar bears, so while resting on the ice they have to be constantly alert.

6 July 1999
79 Nth Fuglehuken

"I have already been in the water for 3/4 of an hour. Every now and then a harbour seal swims by. I think I am going to get out of the water. Or, shall I stay a little longer? Thank God, my waiting was not for nothing! There in all her glory was 'Anabel', a young female harbour seal. She had brought two friends, but these two are so busy with each other, that Anabel and I were left behind. She turned, she left, and she came back again. She circled and disappeared, and suddenly she is right behind me. She rose to the surface, and then met me down below again. Eventually she tentatively touches my outstretched hand, with her snout. She does it again, she left, she came back, and left. It seems that it never stops. She allowed me to hold my hand against her body. Then she brushed up against my hand, as if to be patted. She allows contact with her graceful and soft body. Endlessly this carries on, until she discovered a new game... the same as in the beginning, but this time, when she swims by she grabs my hand with her front flippers and hangs vertically in the water in front of me. It is like we are dancing the Tango at 79 degrees North! A Tango full of passion, which resulted in her grabbing my hand and putting it in her mouth. Eventually we both went to the surface while she was laying with her head in my right arm. A stunning and rare polar memory!"

Robbert Eysink Smeets

The Antarctic

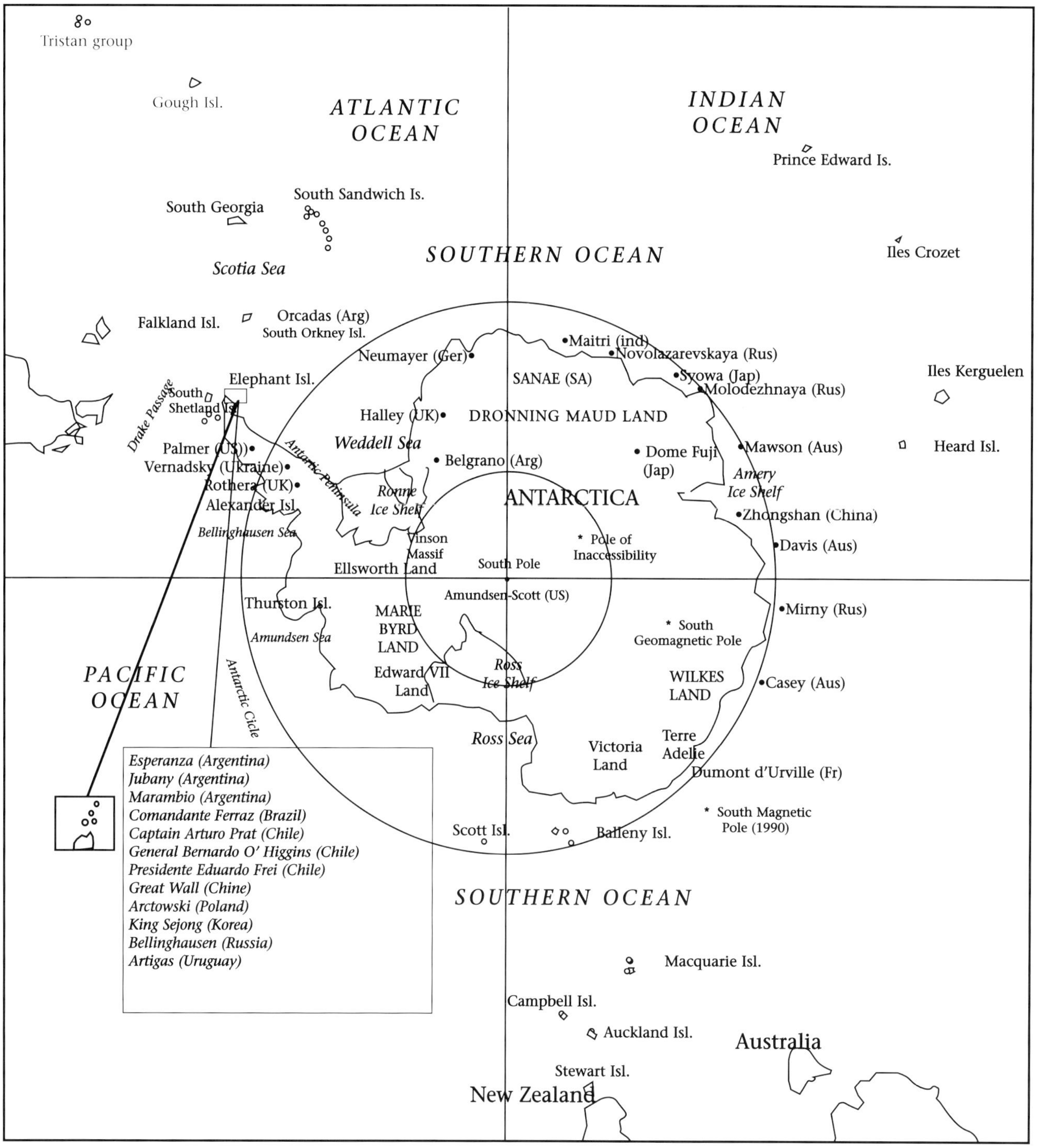

The Antarctic

The Antarctic includes the continent of Antarctica (the fifth largest), the surrounding Southern Ocean, and the peri-Antarctic islands. The northern limit of the Southern Ocean is the Antarctic Convergence.
Antarctica is 99.6% covered by permanent ice and has a surface area of 13.9 million km^2, which includes several massive ice-shelves. The South Pole is 2835 m above sea level, about 2,757 m of which is ice, the surface of this flows about 10 m annually. The average depth of the ice sheet is 2160 m, its maximum recorded depth is 4,76 m at 69.90°S, 135.20°E. This ice has a volume of about 24 million km^3, which is some 90% of that on Earth. Much of the bedrock is depressed below sea level by the weight of the ice sheet; the greatest depression is 2,538 m, at 81°S, 110°W. many peri-Antarctic islands have ice caps, but these are insignificant compared with the continental ice sheet.
Antarctic highest peak is Vinson Massif at 4,897 m (78.58°S, 85.42°W, first climbed on 17 December 1966). The remotest spot is the Southern Pole of Inaccessibility, at 83.83°S, 65.78°E, 1330 km inland.
The Southern Ocean includes the Scotia Sea, Weddell Sea, Amundsen Sea, Ross Sea, and Bellingshausen Sea. Much of it is covered by sea ice which has an average winter maximum area of 20 million km^2 (60% of the Southern Ocean). At the height of summer this decreases top 2 to 4 million km^2 (12% of the ocean). The mean thickness of the ice is 1.2 m; the average duration of a floe is only 1 year.
The first lands seen in the Antarctic were several of the peri-Antarctic islands. Antarctica was first sighted in 1819 and the first landing was in 1821. It was not until 1899 that a winter was spent there and continuous presence began in 1944. The South Pole was reached on 14 December 1911. Sealers, mainly during the 19th century, and whalers during the 20th century were major exploiters of Antarctic resources. Fishing and tourism are the only current commerce, and research is the principal activity. Unlike the Arctic there are neither mining nor transport routes in the Antarctic.
During the 1998 austral winter 43 stations were open in Antarctic regions (25 on Antarctica) recording meteorological data and involved in other scientific research. These were operated by 18 countries. The winter population of the Antarctic is about 1100, at least twice as many are present during the brief summer. The climate is the severest on the planet. Winds often become blizzards and a cold minimum of -89.2°C has been recorded (Earth's lowest). The continent is essentially a frigid desert because there is very little precipitation from the dry air - and virtually all of this is frozen. Terrestrial flora and fauna are highly endemic. They are characterised by few species which may occur in large concentrations. Marine organisms are, on the contrary, abundant in local situations and include many species of whales and commercial fish. The peri-Antarctic islands are particularly important breeding sites for penguins and other sea-birds, and seals. No indigenous humans have existed.
The part of the Antarctic south of 60°C is subject to the Antarctic Treaty of 1959 which has 43 signatory countries (covering 75% of the Earth's population). This places sovereign claims in abeyance and regulates most human activities. Research is co-ordinated by the Scientific Committee on Antarctic Research.

R.K. Headland
Scott Polar Research Institute

Concise chronology of approach to the Antarctic

The following list give explorations, in chronological order, towards the South Pole, their attainment (by sea, air and surface), and the first crossings of the region. There are several claims includes for which supporting evidence is unsatisfactory and doubts exist about their accomplishments.

1603 Gabriel de Castilla (Spain), with a ship's company, probably penetrated the Southern Ocean south of Drake passage. Subsequently several merchant vessels reported being blown south of 60°S rounding Cabo de Hornos in severe weather.

1773 James Cook (Britain), with companies aboard HMS Resolution and HMS Adventure, crossed the Antarctic circle (66.53°S off Dronning Maud Land, 17 January.

1774 James Cook (Britain) on the same expedition reached 71.17°S of Marie Byrd Land, 30 January

1820 Fabian von Bellingshausen (Russia), with companies aboard Vostok and Mirnyy, sighted the Antarctic continent at about 69.35°S off Dronning Maud Land, 27 January.

1823 James Weddell (Britain), with company aboard Jane, reached 74.25°S in the Weddell Sea, 20 February.

1842 James Ross (Britain), with companies aboard HMS Erebus and HMS Terror, reached 78.17°S in the Ross Sea, 23 February.

1900 Hugh Evans (Britain) and 3 others sledged to 78.83°S on the Ross Ice Shelf, 23 February.

1902 Robert Scott (Britain) and 2 others sledged to 82.28°S on the Ross Ice Shelf, 30 December.

1909 Ernest Shackleton (Britain) and 4 others reached 88.38°S, 9 January.

1911 Roald Amundsen (Norway) and 4 others dog-sledged to 90°S, 14 December.

1912 Robert Scott (Britain) and 4 others sledged to 90°S, 17 January (all perished during the return journey).

1929 Richard Byrd (United States), with an aircraft crew, claimed to have flown over the South Pole from the Ross Ice Shelf, 29 November.

1947 Richard Byrd (United States), with crew aboard two aircraft, flew over the South Pole from the Ross Ice Shelf, 15 February.

1956 John Torbert (United States) and 6 others flew across Antarctica over the South Pole (Ross Island to Weddell Sea and returned without landing), 13 January.

1956 Conrad Shinn (United States), with crew of an aircraft, landed at the South Pole, 31 October, a permanent station was then established sustained by aircraft.
Subsequently many aircraft have landed at the South Pole.

1958 Vivian Fuchs (British Commonwealth) and an expeditionary party reached the South Pole with motor vehicles and sledge dogs, 20 January and continued to cross Antarctica (Weddell Sea to Ross Sea).
Subsequently several expeditions have crossed the Antarctic through the South Pole by surface and many have made one-way surface journeys leaving by aircraft.

Johnsons Harbour, a typical settlement in the Falkland Islands.

Black-browed Albatross, *Diomedea melanophrys.* feeds it's chick a piece of squid

Black-browed Albatross, *Diomedea melanophrys,* with the rough west coast of New Island in the background.

Striated Caracara, *Phalcoboenus australis*, (or 'Johnny-Rook') is one of the rarest birds of prey in the world. Its almost restricted to the Falkland Islands

In the Falkland Islands the Long-tailed Meadow Lark, *Sturnella loyca,* accompanies you every where with it's beautiful song.

If the Gentoo Penguin, *Pygoscelis papua*, doesn't watch out, it's most feared predator, the Sub-antarctic Skua, *Catharacta antarctica,* will take it's chance and steal the eggs.

Sometimes Rockhopper Penguins, *Eudyptes chrysocome,* are smashed upon the rocks by the surf, as if they were rubber toys. Once they are on the rocks they continue on their way up to their nesting sites, which sometimes can be 100m high on a steep slope.

The Magellanic Penguin, *Spheniscus magellanicus,* nests in burrows.

The Rockhopper Penguin, *Eudyptes chrysocome,* of Tristan da Cunha, has a more distinctive crest than it's conspecifics in the Falkland Islands.

Tristan da Cunha

'Tristan da Cunha, in the middle of the South Atlantic, is the most isolated inhabited island in the world. It lies 3,000 km west of Cape Town, and 3,300 km east of Buenos Aires. The nearest village is on Saint Helena, 2,460 km to the north. The archipelago also comprises the uninhabited islands Nightingale and Inaccessible, 40 km SW, and Gough Island, 400 km to the SE of Tristan.

Tristan is a circular volcano, with a diameter of 11 km, and a height of 2,067 m. There are very steep cliffs on all sides, up to 300-600 high, which can only be climbed at a few spots. At the foot of the cliff, low plateaus have been formed by secondary eruptions. The largest of these is 6 km long and 600 m wide. This is where the people live, in a village called Edinburgh, but usually referred to as 'The Settlement'. The economy is based on fishing, potatoes, rocklobsters, and postage stamps.

Tristan was discovered in 1506 by the Portuguese Tristão da Cunha, but only became permanently inhabited after 1816, when a British garrison occupied the island. This was to prevent Napoleon, in exile on Saint Helena, from being freed via Tristan da Cunha. The garrison left after one year, but corporal Glass stayed behind, with his wife, a child, and a few bachelor friends. Wives for the friends were imported from Saint Helena. Later, adventurers and shipwrecked sailors joined the group, like the Dutchman Pieter Groen. There are seven surnames nowadays, and everybody is related to everyone.

Tristan has a cool, stormy, and rainy climate, but it never gets really cold. Therefore, the vegetation is almost subtropical. The fauna, however, is subantarctic, and includes fur seals, penguins, albatrosses, and huge numbers of petrels. There are also some unique land birds: three species of finch, a thrush, a flightless moorhen, and a tiny flightless rail.'

Albert Beintema

Yellow-nosed Albatross, *Diomedea chlororhynchos*, at Nightingale Island, in the Tristan group.

White-chinned Petrel, *Procellaria aequinoctialis conspicillata*. The bridled morph is a breeding bird of Tristan da Cunha.

King Penguins, *Aptenodytes patagonica,* at Salisbury Plain, on South Georgia.

'At the beach we were greeted by literally hundreds of King Penguins. They were very inquisitive, walking right up to us. When we sat down they actually came and pulled at our clothing. If we put anything down, they immediately moved towards it and checked it out... any strings were tugged, buttons pecked at, and straps pulled. It was a delight to watch them as they watched us, and at times it was hard to work out who was more interested in the encounter. As we moved away from the beach and further up towards the colony the level of noise increased. There were the standard trumpeting calls that we had heard on the beach, but now there was also the very high pitched peeps and screams of the chicks. It was astonishing to see just how many birds there were, with an estimated 40 thousand pairs, not including all the chicks!'

Ingrid N. Visser

Windy slopes are the perfect nesting site for the Black-browed Albatros *Diomedea melanophrys.*

Grytviken, one of the first Norwegian whaling stations, on South Georgia. In total there were six stations, together with 41 factory ships and 205 catchers. This whole operation was responsible for killing 30,000 whales in just the 1930-31 season.

The melancholy call of the light-mantled Sooty Albatross, *Phoebetria palpebrata,* in the quiet fjords of South Georgia makes the hair on the back of your neck stand up.

A two week old Elephant Seal pup, *Mirounga leonina.*

Young Fur Seal pup, *Arctocephalus gazella.* They were almost extinct at the beginning of the 1900's. Now they are commonly found around the coast of South Georgia.

Wandering Albatross, *Diomedea exulans*, has only one chick every two years. On each foraging trip they may have to travel hundreds of miles to get sufficient food for the chick. From when they leave the nest, until they reach maturity, at six years old, they stay at sea. When they return back to land it is to the natal site. They look for a partner and engage in spectacular displays called 'gamming'.

I am the albatross that waits for you at the end of the earth.

I am the forgotten soul of the dead sailors

who crossed Cape Horn from all the seas of the world.

But they did not die in the furious waves.

Today they fly in my wings to eternity in the last trough of the Antarctic wind.

Sarah Vial

poem inscribed on the albatross sculpture at Cape Horn

One of the best adapted penguins in Antarctica is the Adélie Penguin, *Pygoscelis adeliae.* In the short summer they have to work hard to complete their breeding cycle. Its the Southern most nesting bird in the world.

If you're lucky you can experience Antarctica's beautiful sunsets,
that create these spectacular light effects.
It will give you great photo oppertunities!

Humpback Whales, *Megaptera novaeangliae,* give birth in protected tropical waters, before they take their calves down to Antarctica to feed on the great abundance of krill (shrimp-like creatures).

The chicks of the Chinstrap Penguin, *Pygoscelis antarctica,* are guarded for the first few weeks, by one of the parents, to protect them from predators. Their main distribution is on the South Shetland Islands.

Gentoo Penguins, *Pygoscelis papua*, is a more sub-Antarctic bird, with its southermost breeding sites around the Antarctic Peninsula. It tends to feed more on fish than Adélie Penguin and Chinstrap Penguin.

A top predator in Antarctica, is the Leopard Seal, *Hydrurga leptonyx.* Although it has a bad reputation for killing penguins, it's diet consists mostly of krill.

The Macaroni Penguin, *Eudyptes chrysolophus*, is a rare visitor to the South Shetland Islands.

The unmistakable Cape Petrel, *Daption capense*, is abundant in the southern oceans, and often follows ships.

When most people think of Antarctica, they think of a great continent permanently covered in a huge ice mass, however looking at this picture, taken on Snowhill Island, one should remember that Antarctica is not only ice!